Alexander the Great

Hans Christian Andersen

Aristotle

Johann Sebastian Bach

Ludwig van Beethoven

Alexander Graham Bell

Otto von Bismarck

Simón Bolívar

Johannes Brahms

George Gordon, Lord Byron

Julius Caesar

Enrico Caruso

Mary Cassatt

Catherine the Great

Miguel de Cervantes

Charlie Chaplin

Geoffrey Chaucer

Anton Chekhov

Frédéric Chopin

Winston Churchill

Bill Clinton

Hillary Rodham Clinton

Christopher Columbus

Nicolaus Copernicus

Marie Curie

Salvador Dalí

7

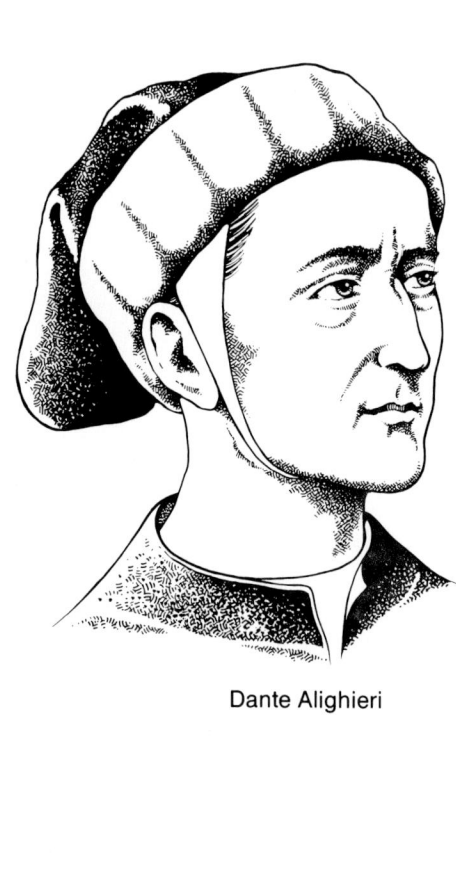

Dante Alighieri

Charles Darwin

Charles Dickens

Emily Dickinson

Dwight D. Eisenhower

Elizabeth I

Henry Ford

Benjamin Franklin

Frederick the Great

Sigmund Freud

Galileo Galilei

Mohandas Gandhi

Charles de Gaulle

George III

Geronimo

George Gershwin

Johann Wolfgang von Goethe

Vincent van Gogh

Ulysses S. Grant

George Frideric Handel

Henry VIII

Adolf Hitler

Henrik Ibsen

Thomas Jefferson

Joan of Arc

Pope John XXIII

Pope John Paul II

Scott Joplin

James Joyce

John Keats

John F. Kennedy

Robert F. Kennedy

Martin Luther King, Jr.

Robert E. Lee

Vladimir I. Lenin

Leonardo da Vinci

Abraham Lincoln

Charles Lindbergh

Franz Liszt

Louis XIV

Martin Luther

Malcolm X

Mao Tse-tung

Marie Antoinette

Karl Marx

Mary, Queen of Scots

Michelangelo Buonarroti

John Milton

Molière (Jean-Baptiste Poquelin)

Wolfgang Amadeus Mozart

Benito Mussolini

Napoleon Buonaparte

Horatio Nelson

Sir Isaac Newton

Friedrich Nietzsche

Florence Nightingale

Eugene O'Neill

23

Louis Pasteur

Peter the Great

Pablo Picasso

Plato

24

Pocahontas

Edgar Allan Poe

Giacomo Puccini

Rembrandt van Rijn

25

Eleanor Roosevelt

Franklin D. Roosevelt

Theodore Roosevelt

Franz Schubert

William Shakespeare

George Bernard Shaw

Percy Bysshe Shelley

Sitting Bull

27

Socrates

Joseph Stalin

Harriet Beecher Stowe

Igor Stravinsky

Peter Tchaikovsky

Mother Teresa

Leo Tolstoy

Harry S Truman

29

Mark Twain

Giuseppe Verdi

Queen Victoria

Voltaire (François-Marie Arouet)

30

Richard Wagner

George Washington

Walt Whitman

Virginia Woolf

Frank Lloyd Wright

Orville Wright

Wilbur Wright